Manage
Your
Stress

Sara Miller McCune founded SAGE Publishing in 1965 to support the dissemination of usable knowledge and educate a global community. SAGE publishes more than 1000 journals and over 800 new books each year, spanning a wide range of subject areas. Our growing selection of library products includes archives, data, case studies and video. SAGE remains majority owned by our founder and after her lifetime will become owned by a charitable trust that secures the company's continued independence.

Los Angeles | London | New Delhi | Singapore | Washington DC | Melbourne

SUPER
QUICK
SKILLS

Manage Your Stress

Learning Centre
Langley College
Station Road
Langley
SL3 8BY

Clare Wilson

Los Angeles | London | New Delhi
Singapore | Washington DC | Melbourne

Los Angeles | London | New Delhi
Singapore | Washington DC | Melbourne

SAGE Publications Ltd
1 Oliver's Yard
55 City Road
London EC1Y 1SP

SAGE Publications Inc.
2455 Teller Road
Thousand Oaks, California 91320

SAGE Publications India Pvt Ltd
B 1/I 1 Mohan Cooperative Industrial Area
Mathura Road
New Delhi 110 044

SAGE Publications Asia-Pacific Pte Ltd
3 Church Street
#10-04 Samsung Hub
Singapore 049483

Editor: Jai Seaman
Assistant editor: Charlotte Bush
Production editor: Tanya Szwarnowska
Proofreader: Brian McDowell
Marketing manager: Catherine Slinn
Cover design: Shaun Mercier
Typeset by: C&M Digitals (P) Ltd, Chennai, India
Printed in the UK

Library of Congress Control Number: 2019944164

British Library Cataloguing in Publication data

A catalogue record for this book is available from
the British Library.

ISBN 978-1-5297-0703-8

Contents

Everything in this book!

Section 1   What's the problem with stress?

When you are stressed, your body triggers the stress response (fight, flight or freeze). If you keep activating the stress response too frequently it can damage your health.

Section 2   Why do I get stressed?

Stressful events are those that are meaningful to you. Understanding the meanings that are important to you can help you manage stress.

Section 3   What are stress mindsets?

The 'Stress is Harmful' mindset includes beliefs that stress must be avoided. The 'Stress is Enhancing' mindset includes beliefs that stress can be enjoyable. Believing a 'Stress is Enhancing' mindset changes your physical stress response, allowing your body to effectively recover.

Section 4 How do I manage my stressful thinking?

Changing our relationship to our thoughts (irrational thoughts or not) by practising self-compassion and meditation reduces stress.

Section 5 How can I directly reduce my feelings of stress?

The four main activity types that turn off the stress response are: physical exercise, creative pursuits, good self-care skills and socializing with others. Progressive muscle relaxation allows you to relax your muscles at will and releases the tension from your body.

Section 6 How do I cope with the stress of other people?

Three main social stresses at university are loneliness, getting annoyed with others and coping with relationship conflict. Understanding what is going on helps you cope.

Section 7 How do I stop procrastinating so I'm no longer stressed?

Procrastination is a form of experiential avoidance (not doing activities that give rise to uncomfortable thoughts or feelings). It is trickier than you think to stop. Start small and reward yourself often. Change the relationship to these thoughts and feelings.

Section 8 How do I develop stress resiliency?

Resiliency is the ability to cope effectively with stress. Using the techniques outlined in this book you should be able to do so.

What's the problem with stress?

10 second summary

In an emergency, stress helps you act fast. However, getting stressed frequently can damage your health.

60 second summary

The stress response (fight, flight or freeze) is the result of interpreting events or situations as being something you cannot cope with. In some situations you need to act fast to keep safe and the stress response helps you do that. However, when the stress response is being activated too often for too long, your health and well-being can be damaged.

Eliminating stress doesn't help because it is not entirely possible to eliminate all stress and you do need to feel stress in urgent situations. Your only choice is to learn to manage stress effectively.

This book will help you develop strategies to do just that.

What is stress?

We experience the physical (e.g., heart racing, palms sweating) and psychological (e.g., worry, can't concentrate) symptoms of stress when we interpret events or situations (e.g., a failed relationship, an assignment deadline looming, no money to catch a bus or getting the flu) as too much to cope with in that moment (e.g., 'I shouldn't have to deal with this', or 'I don't know what to do, I don't believe this is happening!').

Stress Psychological stress is the interpretation of an event, activity or person that you feel you may not be able to adequately cope with, given your current resources. The event, activity or person usually is meaningful to you in some way. Thus, different people are stressed by different events.

How to recognize what causes stress in your life

Have a go at listing ten things you struggle to cope with and you know cause you to experience stress (e.g. deadlines, meeting new people, writing essays, giving a presentation in front of a large audience). Also include activities that you are too afraid to try but would love to.

At the end of this book we will revisit these ten items and come up with effective strategies to deal with each of them.

1 ....

2 ....

3 ....

4 ....

5 ....

6 ....

7 ....

8 ....

9 ....

10 ....

What is the stress response?

When we think we can't cope with these situations (or think we shouldn't have to), the body reacts immediately. The stress response (called the 'fight, flight (flee) or freeze' response) is your body's automatic alarm system:

1 To fight whoever is causing the stress (e.g., other people, small animals, or to put out a fire etc)

2 To take flight, that is, to run away from the situation fast (e.g., from a fire, flood, or any danger that it is safer to see at a distance)

3 To freeze (e.g., play dead so a dangerous animal doesn't take you on, or to stay safe in an earthquake).

Your body's response to stress

To make sure we can take immediate action, the body releases stress hormones which divert energy away from its normal activities of digestion and boosting immunity. When the stress is brief (such as when you get a fright), the hormone epinephrine (adrenalin) is released. Hormones send signals to your organs to tell them what to do, for example, epinephrine tells your heart to start pumping harder. However, when the stress continues (goes on for minutes or hours), the hormone cortisol is released.

Normally, high cortisol signals to your organs to wake up in the morning. However, frequent stress can create high cortisol levels all day, and that can cause a wide range of health problems. For example, the high cortisol levels disrupt digestion (e.g., the sensation of 'butterflies in the stomach' is actually food fermenting in the gut as digestion is disrupted) and can also lower your immunity (increasing the risk of disease). High cortisol levels may also interfere with learning and prevent new memories from being created (making you forgetful).

Hormones A group of molecules that flow into the circulatory system to various organs around the body in order to regulate behaviour or physiology. For example, in stress responses, immediately the hormone epinephrine (adrenalin) is released and then the hormone cortisol is released if the stress persists.

We often misinterpret our bodies. If you are stressed a lot it can seem normal, or you may think you are ill. The student was not allergic to gluten, she was regularly stressed which was the real cause of her sore stomachs (high cortisol may have stopped her digestive system working properly). Luckily the solutions (in this book) were simpler for her to learn than dealing with an allergy.

A student told us

'I thought that I was stressed because I was allergic to gluten and I kept getting a sore stomach.'

Is the solution a stress-free life?

The short answer is no. For example, students who tried to avoid stress over their exam period struggled to concentrate and exercise self-control (Oertig, Schüler, Schnelle, Brandstätter, Roskes, & Elliot, 2013). Further, students who showed the highest increase in epinephrine (adrenalin) during their exams outperformed their calmer classmates (Dienstbier, 1989).

So what can you do?

The rest of this book will outline a number of strategies and techniques that make your life more enjoyable by accurately understanding, managing and using stress to your advantage.

'Stress is the trash of modern life - we all generate it but if you don't dispose of it properly, it will pile up and overtake your life.'

Terri Guillemets

Why do I experience stress?

Try these multiple choice questions to test your understanding. Choose the best response of the three options:

1 Stress is the feelings we get when

   a Bad things happen

   b We interpret something as beyond our control

   c We interpret what is happening to us

2 The stress response is the immediate physiological response of

   a Relax and repair

   b Fight, flight or freeze

   c Find and function

3 Eliminating all stress is not a good idea because

   a It is not possible

   b We cope better with some stress in some situations

   c We would get depressed instead

Congratulations

Now you understand the fact that you experience stress in your whole body! So, any solution needs to include both your mind and body.

Why do I get stressed?

10 second
summary

You often get stressed because
people and activities are meaningful
to you. Recognizing the meaning can
help you deal with stress.

Stress is a good indicator of activities and people who are most meaningful to us. If you are stressed by studying, relationships, or health issues, this is because you care about them. However, often we do not think about our values or the meanings we hold dear. Navigating your stress is easier when you have the clear direction values can provide. You can learn self-affirmations (based on what you value in life) to gain a new perspective on your stress. You can also use self-affirmations (and other techniques) to tolerate (and thereby eliminate) the daily hassles in your life.

How is stress related to meaning?

You get stressed because you want things that are meaningful to you to turn out well. Everything that you care about has the potential to cause you stress (but most things don't cause stress most of the time). For example, if you want to get a good degree, you are likely to be more stressed completing an assignment that contributes to your final mark than one that doesn't.

A student told us

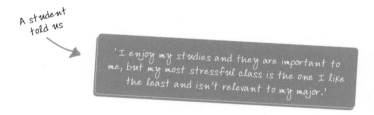

'I enjoy my studies and they are important to me, but my most stressful class is the one I like the least and isn't relevant to my major.'

I explained that it may not be the class per se that was causing the stress. For example, getting a good grade overall may still be important to her (it was) even if the class wasn't. Sometimes what is causing the stress is not immediately obvious.

How do you highlight the meaning in your life?

We often do not think about the various meanings in our lives. Looking at our values is a good way of exploring meaning. Values are directions we choose to go in (e.g., if we value knowledge, we seek out new information). Unlike goals, you never finish your values (at no point do you have all the knowledge), although that value may not be important at another point in your life. Knowing your values can reduce stress dramatically as it gives you a new perspective on what worries you.

Self-affirmation (affirming your values) exercises are very simple, yet powerful techniques that use your values to help you cope with stress. They have also been successfully used in universities to raise students' grades (as it helps students focus on why they are at university).

Values Individual preferences for certain courses of actions, based on what you think is best. For example, thinking being kind to others is an important value may be why you act as a volunteer at a soup kitchen on the weekend.

ACTIVITY How to develop your own self-affirmation story for stress

First, you need to choose three of your top values. Here is a list to help get you thinking:

Adventure	Growth
Beauty	Humour
Compassion	Kindness
Competency	Learning
Creativity	Love
Curiosity	Spirituality
Determination	Success
Friendships	Wisdom

Second, pick one of the three values and write about it for ten minutes. Why is it important to you? Give a detailed example from your past when this value has been particularly important to you. How do you express this value in your life now? Note that values reflect what you care about right now and so this essay is helping you articulate that. You do not need to write about anything stressful, just what is meaningful.

Are daily hassles really an issue?

Actually daily hassles cause more health problems than major life events (as they happen so frequently). Daily hassles seem meaningless. They arise when things do not go our way or events fail to meet our expectations (but annoy us when they block what is meaningful to us). For example, you go to the kitchen to find you are out of food, miss the bus to your lecture so walk and get to the lecture to find that it is an exam which you had forgotten about (eating, getting to your lecture and doing well in an exam are all meaningful). Your stress and frustration when dealing with daily hassles is directly related to your ability to tolerate emotional discomfort. Once you can completely tolerate these emotions they will cease being hassles.

Here are three ways of safely increasing your tolerance to discomfort

1   Allow yourself to regularly feel discomfort. For example, if you really hate feeling fearful, try watching a horror movie (but not before bed) to build up your tolerance. Try listening to Jia Jiang's TEDx MtHood talk *What I learned from 100 days of rejection* or Michelle Poler's TEDx Houston talk *100 days without fear*. These are both successful attempts to increase tolerance to negative emotions by exposure to them.

2   Stay put with the discomfort. For example, if you are worried in an exam, don't leave early even if you have finished. Notice where the discomfort is in your body, and name it (anxiety, or annoyance, or frustration). Not noticing feelings tends to amplify them.

3   Finally, practise welcoming the feeling without creating a story (e.g., 'I shouldn't have to feel this'). The psychologist, Albert Ellis, asked clients to take a banana for a walk around Manhattan on a dog leash. Why? So they could feel foolish, or embarrassed or self-conscious in a fun way and realize the world did not end, and neither did they. Is there a fun way you could do the same?

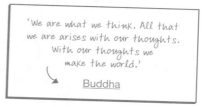

'We are what we think. All that we are arises with our thoughts. With our thoughts we make the world.'

Buddha

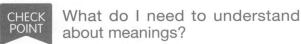

CHECK POINT — ## What do I need to understand about meanings?

Which of the following statements are true:

☐ Values are goals that are meaningful to you.

☐ Values are directions to how you want to live your life.

☐ Self-affirmations are personal values-based stories.

☐ Learning to tolerate emotional discomfort is useless – just ignore what you are feeling.

☐ Tolerating emotional discomfort makes your life easier in the long run as you do not overreact to things.

What are stress mindsets?

10 second summary

Stress mindsets change the way your body reacts to stress.

60 second
summary

Mindsets are a group of beliefs that shape our behaviour. There are two main mindsets about stress. First, the 'Stress is Harmful' mindset is a negative mindset which includes the beliefs that stress must be avoided and stress always damages your health. Second, the 'Stress is Enhancing' mindset is a positive mindset which includes the beliefs that stress can be energizing and enjoyable and allows one to thrive. Believing a 'Stress is Enhancing' rather than a 'Stress is Harmful' mindset changes your physical stress response to the helpful challenge stress response. The latter allows your body to recover effectively, learn and grow with stress rather than being blocked by it.

What are mindsets?

The concept of belief mindsets comes from the work of psychologist Carol Dweck. She was exploring why highly intelligent students were performing poorly. She discovered such students believed that intelligence was fixed (i.e., a fixed mindset) – you were either intelligent or you weren't. Therefore, when problems challenged them, they became very stressed as they assumed they were not intelligent enough to do the task. Other, equally intelligent students successfully completed the problems because they believed that they could learn how to do the problem (that is, they had a growth mindset). Students at university with growth mindsets outperform those with a fixed mindset. Those with a growth mindset believe 'I am a constant learner, and so my abilities are evolving and growing'. Do you?

Mindsets A psychological term for a group of beliefs about you (e.g. your intelligence, or your stress) that influence your behaviour. They tend to be self-fulfilling, as you do not question them and always act accordingly. They are surprisingly easy to change when challenged.

What are stress mindsets?

The set of beliefs we have about stress are called stress mindsets. There are two major mindsets.

1　Stress is terrible, it drains all of my energy and vitality so I can't concentrate or perform well. It should be avoided at all costs (see the problem with avoidance in Section 7). This is the Stress is Harmful mindset.

2　Stress makes me work harder, it gets me out of my bed and helps to focus on what needs to be done. It helps me to work longer and gives me energy. This is the Stress is Enhancing mindset.

How we think influences our biology

For example, twins are walking in the bush and see something on the path ahead. One thinks it is a snake, panics and runs away. The other thinks it is an old rope, and calmly approaches it. Two totally different reactions based on the same situation but resulting from different thoughts.

The Stress is Harmful mindset increases the likelihood that you interpret stress as a THREAT (that is, the traditional fight, flight, freeze stress response discussed in Section 1 with all of its associated problems). There are (hopefully rare) situations that are genuinely threatening and this is the response that can help you deal with them. If such situations happen frequently, your health suffers.

Stress is Harmful is a type of mindset about stress. It is a set of beliefs that stress has many negative attributes (tiring, disrupts learning, decreases performance and increases the likelihood of disease). This mindset is associated with lower well-being than the Stress is Enhancing mindset.

The Stress is Enhancing mindset increases the likelihood that you interpret stress as a CHALLENGE. That is, your cortisol increases as it does in the traditional stress response but other hormones also increase. These hormones, including DHEA (Dehydroepiandrosterone) and oxytocin, protect your body from high cortisol, enhance learning, and increase sociability. It won't surprise you to learn that the challenge stress response is strongly associated with significantly better health outcomes and better well-being (although not less stress).

Stress in Enhancing A type of mindset about stress. It is a set of beliefs that stress has many positive attributes to offer (energizing, engaging, aids learning and improves performance). This mindset is associated with higher well-being and better performance than the Stress is Harmful mindset.

How stress can allow you to rise to a challenge

1 Deal effectively with problems by increasing your energy to

- focus attention

- heighten senses

- increase motivation.

2 Improves relationships with others by activating

- prosocial instincts

- social connections

- social cognition

- increased courage.

3 Helps you learn by encouraging

- nervous system balance

- integration of your experiences

- brain development.

Adapted from McGonigal, K. (2015) *The Upside of Stress: Why stress is good for you (and how to get good at it)*. Vermilion: London.

A student told us

'I understand that it is important to see my need for a high mark as a challenge, but it still feels overwhelming.'

Whilst the mindset is conscious, often the threat vs challenge response is an immediate, unconscious evaluation. Therefore, it is a good idea to practise seeing yourself as capable of learning how to meet some of your stressful challenges so the challenge response becomes more likely.

As the threat response is automatic, it may dominate for a while after you start trying to see the challenge in your stress. The student and I discussed ways he could find some humour in what he was doing and to play with it (he imagined he was teaching someone else his assignment). This allowed the challenge response to take over from the threat response.

Threat Stress Response
The immediately physiological reaction of alarm experienced by the body as fight, flight (flee) or freeze. It prepares the body to take urgent action in the time of a crisis.
It does this by sending energy to the muscles and shutting down 'non urgent' digestive and repair systems.

'The greatest weapon against stress is our ability to choose one thought over another.'

William James

How do the two stress mindsets work with the stress responses?

Complete the flow chart:

A .... mindset

↓

THREAT stress response

↓

The body reacts by

....

....

....

A .... mindset

↓

CHALLENGE stress response

↓

The body reacts by

....

....

....

What can increase your tolerance to daily hassles, which in turn makes it less likely the threat response will turn on?

....

....

How do I manage my stressful thinking?

10 second summary

Challenging irrational beliefs, practising self-compassion and meditating change the way you see your thoughts and relieve them of their stress.

60 second summary

Irrational beliefs are inaccurate beliefs that we have created about ourselves and the world. These can often cause stress as we base our expectations on them. Those expectations tend to then be wrong. Changing our relationship to our thoughts by practising self-compassion and meditation has been shown to not only reduce stress but to also improve learning and concentration.

We have already looked at two techniques to change your stressful thinking (self-affirmations in Section 2 and Stress Mindsets in Section 3). In this section we look at changing irrational beliefs, and changing our relationship to our beliefs (with self-compassion and meditation).

What are irrational beliefs?

Sometimes what is causing our stress is our irrational thinking. A psychologist, Albert Ellis, once wrote that most of the thinking errors he saw in his clients came from three irrational beliefs:

1 To be a worthwhile person, I must achieve everything I set out to achieve (e.g. 'I feel totally worthless, I didn't get the top mark in the class AGAIN').

2 My life's conditions should be easy so I can achieve everything I want without any great effort (e.g. 'I hate going to the library; why isn't all the information online? Lecturers are so lazy making more work for us').

3 Everyone should like me (or, at least treat me well) and if they do not, they should be punished (e.g. 'my tutor group are all a bunch of no-hopers, and yet they complain about me, just because I forgot about our meetings. It is totally unfair').

It is perfectly ok to prefer to be liked, to achieve what you want and to have good life conditions. The problem is if you absolutely expect them and feel it is a catastrophe when things don't go your way.

Irrational Beliefs
Thoughts that are illogical (but appear reasonable to the person believing them). They set up unrealistic expectations and can cause a great deal of stress as they are inaccurate. For example, 'everyone must love me, and if they don't then I am unlovable'.

Once you have recognized irrational beliefs in yourself, start challenging them. Prove them wrong. Laughing at yourself when you think an irrational thought is a great way to start. However, often when we realize we are being irrational, we beat ourselves up and tell ourselves we are stupid.

What is self-compassion?

When we criticize ourselves we can activate our stress response. We think we are helping ourselves by putting ourselves down, but often it is not helpful at all. The antidote to self-criticism is self-compassion. Self-compassion is about being aware we are suffering, realizing that everyone suffers and being kind to ourselves (not judging ourselves so harshly) when we recognize this.

Often we are better at being compassionate towards others than we are to ourselves. One way around this is to think about something about yourself that stresses you in some way. Then imagine receiving a letter advising you about this issue from a very wise old relative you didn't know you had. What would the letter say?

Self-compassion When you are suffering, this is the experience of being kind to yourself, realizing others suffer as well as you and being open to what you are experiencing (accepting any negative emotions associated with your suffering).

What is meditation and how do I do it?

Meditation can also be useful for changing your relationship to your thoughts. Mindfulness mediation has grown in popularity in the last few years, and so there are many courses available both locally and online (as well as mindfulness apps you can try). However, many people misunderstand what meditation is.

A student told us

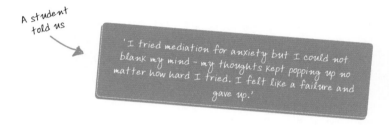

'I tried mediation for anxiety but I could not blank my mind – my thoughts kept popping up no matter how hard I tried. I felt like a failure and gave up.'

It is not the content of your mind (blank or full of thoughts) that is important, but rather your awareness of the content. Meditation is a way of being in relationship to the present moment (including your present moment thoughts and feelings and life). So, if you are angry or anxious or depressed, then that is what you are within that moment. It is not an escape from present problems, so it will not always be relaxing. The student had been successfully meditating all along. Once he realized that, he started a regular practice and over time his reactivity to anxiety reduced considerably. With practice, you do also improve your concentration and learning.

Meditation A broad term that covers a range of practices that change your relationship to your thoughts and feelings. These practices usually involve the development of focus and attentional skills. They work best when practised daily.

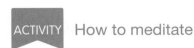

ACTIVITY How to meditate

One of my favourite meditations is simply to close your eyes, sit comfortably and listen. Listen to all the sounds of life going on around you as if it were an orchestra, a piece of music. Let those sounds and silences wash over you, don't try and judge them. You will find yourself distracted and carried off with your thoughts and that's absolutely fine; as soon as you realize come back to listening to them as if they were music. If you can do this for five minutes at a time, wonderful. Over time you can build up to 30 minutes a day if you fancy it.

> 'The greatest mistake you can make in life is to be continually fearing you will make one.'
>
> Elbert Hubbard

What changes my stressful thinking?

A quick quiz to test your knowledge:

1 Below is a list of stressful beliefs. Choose which of the three
   irrational beliefs on p.46 most likely form the basis of each of these
   comments:

☐ I have to study harder than other students just to keep up, it's
   totally unfair.

☐ That lecturer just doesn't like me, we have never met but I can
   tell by the way she looks at me.

☐ I know I deserve a much higher mark than I got; I don't
   think the lecturer understands how hard I worked on that
   assignment.

☐ That postgraduate course is really hard to get on to, and if I
   don't get in my life is over.

2 How can self-compassion help relieve stress?

....

....

....

....

....

....

....

....

3 How can meditation help relieve stress?

....

....

....

....

....

....

....

....

Congratulations

Terrific!

You should now know that your thinking plays a prominent role in stress... but you can change your mind!

How can I directly reduce my feelings of stress?

10 second summary

Engaging in positive physical activities relaxes the body beautifully. Teaching yourself progressive muscle relaxation can also help you relax.

60 second
summary

The four main activity types that reduce cortisol and turn off the stress response are: physical exercise (walking is one of the best for relaxation but more cardio exercise also helps); creative pursuits (music is particularly good but any can be effective if you enjoy doing it); good self-care skills (a good night's sleep is one of the best but a good quality diet is often neglected); and socializing with others (particularly people you love). Further, progressive muscle relaxation is cheap (free) and easy to learn. It allows you to relax your muscles at will and releases the tension from your body.

What physical activities can help me relax?

There are a number of activities that have been shown to turn off the stress response, primarily by reducing your cortisol levels and relaxing you. They can be grouped into four types:

1 **Physical Exercise:**

- Go for a walk
- Go to the beach
- Walk around your neighbourhood, shopping centre, or forest
- Dance around your room
- Practise yoga or tai chi
- Take slow deep breaths into your belly.

2 **Creativity:**

- Take up a hobby (knitting, football)
- Sing (by yourself, or for an added boost, with others e.g., in a choir or pop group) or listen to music; play a musical instrument
- Laugh (save the links to a range of funny YouTube videos so you have something to laugh at when you need to).

3 **Self-Care:**

- Have a long hot bath
- Eat food that nourishes you (note: cortisol increases your appetite so try to relax before you eat)
- Get plenty of sleep (lack of sleep also increases cortisol)
- Exercise.

4 **Socializing:**

- Play with your pet (if you like animals but don't have a pet, why not volunteer at a local animal shelter?)

- Go out with friends (e.g. dancing, go to an exciting or funny movie)

- Call your parents for a chat.

A student told us

'I don't have time to do all of these activities, as they just feel like I'm avoiding getting my dissertation finished.'

Often when you most need to take a break is when you least think you need to take a break. Many students think it is better to study throughout the night rather than get some sleep. However, for your learning, health and stress levels, eight hours of sleep is vastly superior to an all-nighter. The student and I discussed how important it was to get some distance from her dissertation and to take regular breaks to exercise and look after herself. Much to her surprise she discovered the dissertation was easier to write when she was less stressed and well-rested.

There is also a simple technique that you can also use to reduce stress: Progressive Muscle Relaxation.

What is Progressive Muscle Relaxation and how do I do it?

Progressive Muscle Relaxation was first devised by Edmund Jacobson in the early 1900s. It is still practised today because it is simple, easy to learn, and once the technique is learnt, it is very effective at relaxing you whenever you want (especially for people who hold tension in their bodies when they are stressed). The basic technique is to clench a small group of muscles (e.g., both hands clenched into a fist) as you inhale, then you hold both your breath and the muscles for up to 10 seconds (to really feel the tension in your muscles) and next you relax the muscles as you breath out for up to 10 seconds (to feel the relaxation that replaces the tension). You do this for all the muscle groups of your body. It is best to start with your feet (e.g. curl up your toes) then move up the body.

If you would prefer to listen to someone instructing you on what to do, there are many videos online. Alternatively you could record your own script on your mobile (there are also scripts online, just search for 'Progressive Muscle Relaxation scripts'). You should practise Progressive Muscle Relaxation twice a day (first thing in the morning, and last thing at night) for at least 14 days (so you will be more aware

Progressive Muscle Relaxation A series of muscle exercises. Each muscle in the body goes through a set sequence of tightening, holding and then releasing. If practised regularly for a week or two, you can easily learn to release tension from your body.

of when tension gathers in your muscles and you are able to then immediately release this tension whenever you need to). You may find that in the future just doing the fist clench can remind your body to relax all over.

'Tension is who you think you should be. Relaxation is who you are.'

Chinese proverb

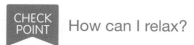 How can I relax?

Tick the items below that can aid relaxation:

☐ Shaking your body

☐ Dancing

☐ Sitting still for hours

☐ Playing a musical instrument

☐ Judging your musical performance

☐ Staying out all night

☐ Taking a hot bath

☐ Spending time with friends

☐ Phoning a call centre

☐ Calling your parents

How do I cope with the stress of other people?

10 second summary

Loneliness is a feeling that most people experience at university. We get annoyed with others because our expectations of them may be unrealistic.

Other people can be a great source of joy but, because they mean so much to us, they can also cause the greatest stress. Three main social stresses at university are loneliness, getting annoyed with others and coping with relationship conflict. Loneliness can be a source of stress at university, particularly if you think you are the only one who is lonely. Knowing most people get lonely can help. Sometimes fellow students and friends can let us down, usually because a) we expected things that were unrealistic, or b) the people did not know what our expectations were. Conflict can also cause a great deal of stress and it is important to treat people with respect when you are in dispute with them.

How to handle loneliness

The stereotype of the lonely person is the 'weird loser who has no friends'. However, most people are lonely at some point at university. It is in big, crowded spaces that most people can feel the loneliest (and stressed about it) because they think they shouldn't be. Here are three tips on reducing your loneliness:

1   Recognize that loneliness is a feeling not a fact. That is, just because you feel lonely does not mean you are truly alone. Be kind to yourself and know that feelings pass.

2   Recognize that you are not alone in your loneliness, so try every day to talk to other people in your classes or around the university who may be feeling as lonely as you. You could make their day.

3   Be persistent. It may feel awkward trying to meet new people, but keep trying. Knowing how to reduce your loneliness is a great skill you will use for the rest of your life. However, if you are struggling, please seek professional help from your university's student support services.

People are annoying

At university, you can spend much of your time with friends and you can develop high expectations about how you think they should behave. This can lead to conflict when their expectations of themselves do not match yours. Sometimes just knowing that it is unrealistic to expect others to meet your expectations is enough to calm the annoyance you may feel towards them. If that isn't enough, step back and look at the relationship as objectively as you can, asking yourself the following questions:

- Is the aspect that is annoying you something they are doing?

  Perhaps ask them about it, but know that while you are entitled to ask someone to do things differently, they can refuse your request.

- If not, is it something you think they did?

  Many of the student conflicts I have dealt with were concerned with what one student thought another student did, and often the student was wrong.

- Is there something you could change that would in turn reduce the annoying behaviour (or your perception of the behaviour)?

  For example, if you are annoyed that a friend doesn't turn up to lectures but expects your notes, why not ask them to take notes for you (or find out why they are not turning up to the lecture – is it something that they need help with?)

Conflict in relationships

Psychologist John Gottman describes four behaviours he calls the 'Four Horsemen of the Apocalypse' because they usually signal marriages are about to break apart. In my experience, these behaviours are also often present in tutorial groups and group work. It may be a good idea to learn how to avoid them now so none of your relationships (with colleagues, friends, or partners) need feature them:

1   Criticism of the person, rather than an aspect of their behaviour that you object to. Instead of saying to a fellow group member 'you're totally lazy', try 'as a group we need you to do your share of the assignment by the deadline.'

2   Showing contempt towards the person by mocking them, name-calling, looking them up and down or eye-rolling. This is often seen as a form of bullying. Instead of eye-rolling, try looking at your computer until you can calmly glance up at them.

3   Getting defensive towards the person if they complain about you. Instead of angrily replying to a complaint with 'well, what about you....', try paraphrasing what they said and say you need to think about it and will get back to them.

4   Stonewalling a person by totally ignoring them. This is one of the most toxic. Instead of ignoring the person, try 'I am really upset with you at the minute. I will get back to you when I have calmed down.'

A student told us

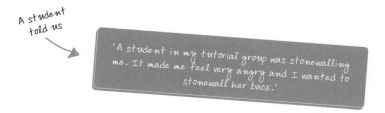

'A student in my tutorial group was stonewalling me. It made me feel very angry and I wanted to stonewall her back.'

Often when someone is hurting us we want to hurt them back. That rarely solves anything. Further, we are often told to 'just ignore them'. However, it is better to try and talk to them as a first step. It may not work but at least you know you tried.

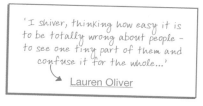

'I shiver, thinking how easy it is to be totally wrong about people – to see one tiny part of them and confuse it for the whole...'

Lauren Oliver

 How did you do?

Name three tips for handling loneliness:

1

2

3

What are the four behaviours that can cause trouble in relationships?

1

2

3

4

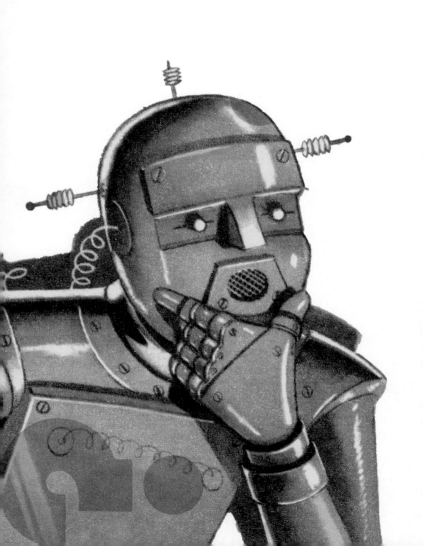

How do I stop procrastinating so I'm no longer stressed?

10 second summary

Avoidance (including procrastination) can undermine your study habits and your mental health.

Experiential avoidance is the practice of not doing activities because you want to avoid feeling feelings, or thinking thoughts that are uncomfortable. This feels great at the time. However, it increases the likelihood we will avoid again in the future. So we do. Then when we try to do whatever we were avoiding, it has become a real struggle. Although everyone avoids sometimes, it is a great idea not to do so too often. If you find yourself procrastinating frequently it is a good idea to start small and to reward yourself frequently as this may help you overcome the problem.

What is experiential avoidance?

There are plenty of distractions to help students avoid studying. For example, 'I need to study for the exam, but I don't feel like it so I'm off to the pub'; or 'I don't understand the assignment at all but I hate feeling embarrassed so I am not going to ask anyone for help.' When you avoid something because you don't want to experience negative thoughts or feelings (e.g., anxiety or embarrassment), you get a sense of relief (e.g., the pub is more enjoyable than you thought studying would be). This sense of relief is called negative reinforcement and helps your brain to learn that the avoidance activity (the pub) is a good thing to repeat. So you avoid the activity again.

However, when you try to do the activity you avoided, you may struggle. For example, 'I sat down to do my assignment and I felt sick. I have no idea what's wrong with me; I felt fine ten minutes ago'; or 'I went to ask the tutor about the assignment, and my mind went blank. I just asked the stupidest of things'. This is very stressful. You taught your brain (consciously or otherwise) that this thing you are avoiding is REALLY bad. In reality it isn't. In reality, you are more than capable of coping with it. But you have convinced yourself you can't by avoiding it. It isn't a small problem. High levels of avoidance predict most mental health problems (including depression and anxiety), and high stress.

Negative reinforcement when you are more likely to do a behaviour if it reduces the likelihood of something aversive. For example, you feel anxious about an exam so you get drunk. Getting drunk reduces the anxiety so you are more likely to drink when anxious in the future.

Experiential Avoidance Not doing something because you want to avoid the thoughts, feelings, memories or physical sensations associated with the activity. For example, 'I would start my assignment, but I don't feel like it (that is, I feel uncomfortable so I would rather do something else that feels more comfortable).'

A student told us

'I was going to withdraw from university because I seemed to have lost my ability to write assignments. I used to enjoy them and now I can't even get started.'

This is not uncommon, and it can feel like you are incompetent. However, the student and I discussed how avoidance can trick one into feeling this way, and how small steps and regular rewards may get his writing mojo back. It worked and although it was a struggle, he completed his degree.

A common form of experiential avoidance in students is procrastination and it is not easy to overcome. For example, perhaps you often procrastinate about starting your assignments, so you do the following: You set four hours aside today to complete that assignment. You start enthusiastically and spend three hours straight working on it. You are thrilled. You don't usually spend three hours working straight and you are now more than halfway through. Unfortunately, this pattern may train you to procrastinate more in the future.

What's the problem?

Well, actually there are three problems:

1. You started working because you felt excited about doing so. Teaching yourself to only study when you feel like it can make your life very stressful, which in turn reduces the likelihood you will feel like it.

2. Four hours working was never realistic, even three hours is a long time to concentrate. Setting unrealistic goals will cause stress and a sense of failure even when you did a good job. Failing at overcoming avoidance makes you less likely try again.

3. Deciding in advance it will take x- amount of time can cause unnecessary stress when you really do not know how long it will take.

The best strategies to deal with avoidance are the following

1   Start out by making small changes, so small that they are really easy
    for you to do (that way you do not need to 'feel good' to start with).
    For example, if you have a semester to complete an assignment,
    spend up to 20 minutes each day working on it. The important point
    is to STOP after 20 minutes, so you work based on the time, not on
    your feelings.

2   Give yourself a small reward immediately after you complete the
    small change for the day. For example, once you complete your
    20 minutes, congratulate yourself (praising yourself can work
    wonders).

3   Make sure you focus on the process, not the outcome. You have
    control over how much you work and its quality but you do not have
    control over who grades your work or your mark. If you know you
    did your best you will experience less stress whatever the grade.

4   If you struggle with negative thoughts or feelings, then review
    Section 4, as changing your relationship to any negative thoughts
    and feelings may help you overcome your avoidance (see also daily
    hassles in Section 2).

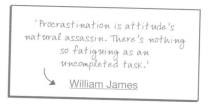

'Procrastination is attitude's
natural assassin. There's nothing
so fatiguing as an
uncompleted task.'

William James

CHECK POINT What is avoidance?

Below is a series of statements about avoidance. Which are true?

1 Avoidance feels good which is why you want
to do it again... True / False

2 Avoidance (including procrastination) is not
linked to mental health problems at all..................... True / False

3 Avoidance is easy to overcome, you just do
what you want to do.. True / False

4 Rewarding yourself when you do not avoid
is a good way to prevent avoidance......................... True / False

5 Rewarding yourself for whatever you do is good.......... True / False

Congratulations

Marvelous! You should now be mindful that meeting people and moving helps reduce stress, whereas avoiding these things doesn't.

How do I develop stress resiliency?

10 second summary

Resiliency is built on choosing a range of techniques to practise and use regularly to manage stress effectively.

60 second summary

Resiliency is the ability to cope effectively with stress. When coping with stress there are four options: change the cause of stress; learn relaxation techniques; learn thought management techniques; and prevention. Using techniques such as meditation and a 'Stress is Enhancing' mindset to practise regularly as part of a prevention programme allows your stress to be experienced as a challenge rather than as a threat. Further, making goals that are larger than yourself and taking different perspectives on your life can help to maintain your psychological well-being. Together these build a psychological resiliency tool kit that you can use to live effectively with stress and enhance your life.

What is resiliency?

Resiliency is the ability to cope with a crisis and to recover from any stress.

With any stressful situation there are four possible areas to find the best way to cope:

1. Change the activity causing the stress. For example, finish the essay, sort out your study skills, or ask your tutor for help.

2. Relaxation exercises. For example, physical exercise or progressive muscle relaxation.

3. Thought management. For example, adopt a stress mindset of Stress is Enhancing or challenging irrational beliefs.

4. Prevention. For example, meditation or all of the above but done regularly rather than only in response to a stressful situation.

The most successful of the four is prevention. Any resiliency tool kit will work best if prevention is its focus. Here is an example from a former student: ring mum once a week; catch up with my friends at least once a day (in person if possible); walk to uni (unless it is raining, then take the bus); go to library for an hour before my first lecture and work on assignments (read self-affirmation first, or write a new one); set realistic small goals each day and reward myself immediately (Tetris). Notice when I start to feel stress, and think how I can make it enhancing (butterflies are giving me energy to get done what I need to do); meditate each night for 20 minutes; get eight hours of sleep.

Resiliency Your ability to cope and adapt, particularly to trauma and stress. The higher the resiliency you experience, the lower the likelihood you will experience the threat stress response. Those who are high in resiliency in a given situation experience greater well-being than those lower in resiliency.

A student told us

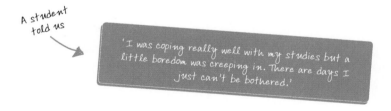

'I was coping really well with my studies but a little boredom was creeping in. There are days I just can't be bothered.'

Boredom is also part of life. However, sometimes a possible solution is to reframe your goals 'bigger-than-yourself' and this can help you see a more meaningful picture. For example, his goal was to become a teacher (which is about him), so we reframed that as helping children to develop a love of learning (same goal but about others). This helped him to feel less alone and more part of his community.

Finally, a totally different perspective

We often think life isn't being fair to us and that our stress is not what we should have to cope with. We might become resentful or bitter. Here is a little playful thought exercise from the philosopher Alan Watts (from his lecture, The Dream of Life) that might give you another perspective on your troubles. (He gave this lecture in the 1960s so his language is of its time). It goes like this:

Imagine that, when you're asleep, you can dream about anything you want to dream, for any length of time. To start with, you would give yourself anything you could wish for, but after a while, you might start to want something unknown and out of your control. As Alan Watts says:

You would dig that and would come out of that and you would say 'Wow that was a close shave, wasn't it?' Then you would get more and more adventurous and you would make further- and further-out gambles as to what you would dream. And finally, you would dream where you are now. You would dream the dream of living the life that you are actually living today.

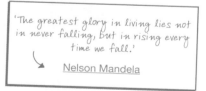

'The greatest glory in living lies not in never falling, but in rising every time we fall.'

Nelson Mandela

How do I change my top ten stresses?

Go back to Section 1 and recall your top ten stresses. Now fill in the table below:

Do I change the cause of the stress; relax, change my thinking, or work on prevention?

Name of stress	Preferred technique to help	How regularly do I need to practise this	Timeline to do so

Final checklist: How to know you are done

Do you understand what stress is?............................... Yes / No

Do you know what the stress response is?..................... Yes / No

Can you identify three things you can do to tolerate
emotional discomfort?... Yes / No

Do you know what self-affirmations are and
how they can be used?... Yes / No

Do you know what meditation is? .... Yes / No

Do you know three ways you can develop a
Stress is Enhancing mindset?................................... Yes / No

Do you understand how you can manage your
stressful thinking effectively?..................................... Yes / No

Have you created a list of 'go-to' activities to
use when you are stressed?..................................... Yes / No

If someone you know said they were feeling lonely,
do you know what advice you would give them?.............. Yes / No

Do you know what experiential avoidance is?................. Yes / No

Do you know the best way to handle avoidance?............. Yes / No

Have you created a stress resiliency tool kit?.................. Yes / No

Glossary

Experiential Avoidance   This is not doing something because you want to avoid the thoughts, feelings, memories or physical sensations associated with the activity. For example, 'I would start my assignment, but I don't feel like it (that is, I feel uncomfortable so I would rather do something else that feels more comfortable)'.

Hormones   These are a group of molecules that flow into the circulatory system to various organs around the body in order to regulate behaviour or physiology. For example, in stress responses, immediately the hormone epinephrine (adrenalin) is released and then the hormone cortisol is released if the stress persists.

Irrational beliefs   These are thoughts that are illogical (but appear reasonable to the person believing them). They set up unrealistic expectations and can cause a great deal of stress as they are inaccurate. For example, 'everyone must love me, and if they don't then I am unlovable.'

Meditation   This is a broad term that covers a range of practices that change your relationship to your thoughts and feelings. These practices usually involve the development of focus and attentional skills. They work best when practised daily.

Mindsets   A mindset is a psychological term for a group of beliefs about you (e.g. your intelligence, or your stress) that influence your behaviour. They tend to be self-fulfilling, as you do not question them and always act accordingly. They are surprisingly easy to change when challenged.

Stress is Enhancing   This is a type of mindset about stress. It is a set of beliefs that stress has many positive attributes to offer (energizing, engaging, aids learning and improves performance). This mindset is associated with higher well-being and better performance than the Stress is Harmful mindset.

Stress is Harmful   This is a type of mindset about stress. It is a set of beliefs that stress has many negative attributes (tiring, disrupts learning, decreases performance and increases the likelihood of disease). This mindset is associated with lower well-being than the Stress is Enhancing mindset.

Negative reinforcement   Negative reinforcement is when you are more likely to do a behaviour if it reduces the likelihood of something aversive. For example, you feel anxious about an exam so you get drunk. Getting drunk reduces the anxiety so you are more likely to drink when anxious in the future.

Progressive Muscle Relaxation   This is a series of muscle exercises. Each muscle in the body goes through a set sequence of tightening, holding and then releasing. If practised regularly for a week or two, you can easily learn to release tension from your body.

Resiliency   This is your ability to cope and adapt, particularly to trauma and stress. The higher the resiliency you experience, the lower the likelihood you will experience the threat stress response. Those who are high in resiliency in a given situation experience higher well-being than those lower in resiliency.

Self-compassion   When you are suffering, this is the experience of being kind to yourself, realizing others suffer as well as you and being open to what you are experiencing (accepting any negative emotions associated with your suffering).

Stress   Psychological Stress is the interpretation of an event, activity or person that you feel you may not be able to adequately cope with, given your current resources. The event, activity or person usually is meaningful to you in some way. Thus, different people are stressed by different events.

Threat Stress Response   This is the immediately physiological reaction of alarm experienced by the body as fight, flight (flee) or freeze. It prepares the body to take urgent action in the time of a crisis. It does this by sending energy to the muscles and shutting down 'non urgent' digestive and repair systems.

Challenge Stress Response   This is a similar system to the threat response in that it does prepare the body for action. However, it does not prepare for an emergency, but rather for a high level of activity (such to play, or to learn) that may require effort, concentration and creativity.

Values   These are individual preferences for certain courses of action, based on what you think is best. For example, thinking being kind to others is an important value may be why you act as a volunteer at a soup kitchen on the weekend.

References, further reading and resources

Resources for more information about stress

American Institute of Stress: www.stress.org

Mind: www.mind.org.uk/information-support/types-of-mental-health-problems/stress/#.XVZtEvkzYhs

Self-compassion: https://self-compassion.org/

References

Crum, A, J., Salovey, P., Achor, S. (2013). Rethinking stress: The role of mind-sets in determining the stress response. *Journal of Personality and Social Psychology, 104*(4), 716–733.

Dienstbier, R. A. (1989). Arousal and physiological toughness: Implications for mental and physical health. *Psychological Review, 96*(1), 84–100.

McGonigal, K. (2015). *The Upside of Stress: Why stress is good for you (and how to get good at it)*. Vermilion: London.

NHS. How to deal with stress. Available at: www.nhs.uk/conditions/stress-anxiety-depression/understanding-stress

Oertig, D., Schüler, J., Schnelle, J., Brandstätter, V., Roskes, M., & Elliot, A. J. (2013). Avoidance of goal pursuit depletes self-regulatory resources. *Journal of Personality, 81*(4), 365–375.

Strack, J., & Esteves, F. (2014). Exams? Why worry? The relationship between interpreting anxiety as facilitative, stress appraisals, emotional exhaustion, and academic performance. *Anxiety, Stress, and Coping: An International Journal,* 1–10.

Apps

These can be great. (If you look for stress know that most treat that as anxiety). The best ones for you will be ones that you choose to best suit your lifestyle. For meditation and relaxation, try: Headspace, Happify, Breathe2relax and Stop, Breathe & Think.

Further psychological help

Sometimes we need people to help us. If you feel you would like to talk to a professional about any issues that may have been raised by this book, please consider contacting your doctor to discuss what options are best for you, or your university Student Support Services (they usually have excellent counselling services available).